Lost Lullaby

Patrick Harte

ORIGINAL WRITING

© 2011 Patrick Harte

All rights reserved. No part of this publication may be reproduced in any form or by any means—graphic, electronic or mechanical, including photocopying, recording, taping or information storage and retrieval systems—without the prior written permission of the author.

ISBN: 978-1-908282-44-6

A CIP catalogue for this book is available from the National Library.

Published by ORIGINAL WRITING LTD., Dublin, 2011.

Printed in Great Britain by MPG BOOKS GROUP,
Bodmin and Kings Lynn

In memory of my late father and mother
John and Teresa

I would like to say a special thanks to Dr Eileen Doyle for the proof reading of my poems and her kind encouragement.

Contents

Section I

LOST LULLABY	1
CLASHAGANNY DAWN	2
LAMENT	3
NETTLES	4
THE TRIALS OF OSCAR	5
TROUT	6
WORDS	7
TICKING CLOCKS	9

Section II

SERVES TWO	13
FATHER OF FOUR	14
FOX	16
RYAN'S MILLTOWN	17
SEESAW	18
THE POTTER'S WHEEL	20
SPRING	21
AFTERLIFE	22

Section III

WITHERING AWAY	27
GEM	28
MEMORIES	29
AND MOTHER NEVER CRIED	30
LIFE	32
DAYS END	33
PARTING	34
RESTING PLACES	35

Section IV

HER PYRAMID	39
1941	40
PROFOUND PASTIMES	41
HOUSEMARTINS	43
NEW CUT GRASS	44
THE MILLRACE	45
YOU ARE	46

Section V

SHADOWS FALL	51
CRASS CREASE AND CROWN	52
LIFEFORCE	54
LAST SUMMER	55
THE DANCE	56
TO A STRANGER	57
EVENING TIME	58

Lost Lullaby

Section I

Lost Lullaby

I watch with a cloying, silent, agony
At life's sieved existence, sleeping gently,
Catapulting my isolation to deeper darkness.

Outside, autumn, too, is claiming back the light,
Eavesdropping on every turning leaf and rattled shoot,
A kind of truce, a sensory holocaust.

There is now only a kind of waiting, and yet
Each is prepared but not yet ready.
There will be no rest this night.

I have come full circle on myself
Singing my life's lost lullaby, but, I am weeping,
Who will call me son now?

Clashaganny Dawn

I awake and smell the morning's breath
In a Clashaganny dawn
The swell of the morning rises over me
And I am born

Into the mysteries of all greening things
Riotous, lushful and sprung
Headlong chasing the turning tide
It has begun

To whisper softly what must be achieved
Metered, measured and teased
Backslapping the months as they fall behind
I fall to my knees

To watch the flies butter the heady air
On their clipped and twirling flight
A symphony on a garden plant
Combust and ignite

The dying embers of a season's end
Recalled to their birthing place
To push through and creep across
Earth's shaven face

LAMENT

Man's a little box of tinder,
Shuffling around with scant regard,
Unknown here, return to sender,
Failure is currency to discard,
And yet, he promises what he preaches,
Sea-change at a single stroke,
Wringing his hands, he overreaches,
Arrogant as always, he goes for broke.

Nettles

In bullying clumps and summer swagger glare
Nettles bristle caution -
And needle-fury if rubbed up the wrong way.

Each wiry stem and rip saw leaf
Pressing aggression, pain volleyed weapons
Poised for that lighter touch.

Their triggers cocked, exploding silent fury
Into the flesh, a stabbing frenzy unleashed.
Each one injecting retaliation.

And now they signal their retreat-
Dying back. Servants to the seasons,
Re-arming. Rising with a new ferocity.

The Trials Of Oscar

When kissing the youthful lips he sealed
His fate, his life, his history.
The passion that spilt forth suddenly revealed
A fiery world, a ruinous trajectory.

Brilliant, bright light, razor wit edge
Flared up, exploded, then fell.
Forged in a ballad, declaring his rage,
Pared down and poised for Dante's hell.

Seated in Merrion, most quoted of men.
The streets now rejoice and sing.
With the tables now turned three fifty and ten,
His resurrection complete, his importance re-turning.

Trout

There among the frothy bubbles he hangs
Motionless, silent, weightless,
The fighter waiting to fight,
The swimmer waiting to swim,
The leaper waiting to leap.
I tied up with all my glory
The mystery of this watery place
Where the silence is your gillie
And the world is far away
For this shootout there is no shining steel
Only carbon, line and fly.
No one will know the outcome
Someone will have to die
I stalked him like an assassin
Along the margins of his world
Where place and pace are paramount
To the catcher's eye unfurled
Feather light grey duster
The surface tension holds
Proud mimickery of an ancient life
The torpedo rises and rolls….

Words

I find them gathered on a lonely shelf
Bound together with the I and the self

I find them in the modes of conversation
Cross fertilising dialects in copulation

I find them litigating in open court
With eloquence unravelling aggravated hurt

I find them in the lover's embrace
Wild abandon about them hurriedly chase

I find them spinning in some battlefield
Vitriolic shelling obliterates need

I find them in the art of creation
Mining for that spark of inspiration

I find them bloated in a bad situation
Misshapen, twisted in retaliation

I find them in an autumn leaf turned gold
Gathered into nature's motherly hold

I find them in the quiet idle time
Resting with their backs against mine

I find them brilliant that we should know
From their birth they continue to flow

Ticking Clocks

As I listened intently to ticking clocks
Tick-tocking away at time's measured blocks,
Sculpting the lines on that chiselled face,
Watching precious moments balance time and place.

I look into the mirror at times unrest
And view the only loser in this contest,
The up and down rhythm and rhyme we keep,
Some of us will laugh and some will weep.

But time with all its measuring tools
Passes right on by the waiting fools,
It seems to me lest we forget
The self in motion knows no regret.

Section II

Serves Two

My fingers move across the page
Virgin white and unstained,
Together we will consummate
Flights of fancy unrestrained.

And as I search for new recruits
To fill the holding lines,
Something new finds aptitude
Comes together in glowing rhymes.

Cold words assembled in ordered rows
March with a measured ease,
Formations indisputable
Their only aim to please.

Father Of Four

A brace of birds on the kitchen table
A Sunday shot at dawn
Old fashioned, maybe, hard of hand
Flat-capped pate, brawn

Father of four you did your best
You gave us your life and all the rest
But life has been cruel and changed all the rules
Nowadays society would only point and ridicule

Taciturn tortured your words went to ground
To wait out the hunter's beat
Perplexed by the chatter of wasted words
When a simple yes or no would replete

Father of four that was your lot
You carried on like there was no could not
But life will do to you just what it pleases
Its contemptuous nature mocks and jeers us

Countersunk and tightened into place
Your emotions never betrayed you
Oh come on now and give us a clue
A hint, a brief sneak preview

Father of four it's all over now
We look back and we say how
But life cannot stop what you set in motion
Four go forward with your sense of proportion

Fox

I understand now your nightly calls
Around my house your silent paws

Mooching through with darkened hope
'Til morning arcs its gentle slope

No trace of red, no searching eyes
Phantom dog of the countryside

Hell and hound runs through your veins
A whipping boy, red rural stains

But through it all you held your ground
The hunter's cry, the bugle sound

It's good to know while safe in bed
The hunted is hunting in my head

Ryan's Milltown

Holding court like a senior wig
He counters quick wit with tit for tat sorties
Into the blue maelstrom like a squealing pig

Released to chase at a country fair.
Battle-lines drawn, they respond in kind,
Sniping from the high chair,

The rising pitch oscillates, smelting bygone
Days into little scenes, marbling the mind.
Which was a time he always looked upon?

With an open heart, a time to unwind.

Seesaw

I know that life is fast
Everyday it races past
The mind first, the body last

There is no me in aspiration
Juxtaposition with this isolation
Holding my breath in anticipation

There's always something better over there
But I always go elsewhere
Now who told you life was fair

I was undefeated 'til now
They got me on the ropes somehow
But I bounced back and took a bow

I stood when I should have sat
The body now reminds me of that
I swallowed when I should have spat

I am a single minded man
That follows through with a plan
Do best what best you can

It's like sitting in life's great maw
With no where left to withdraw
Existence is the great seesaw

The Potter's Wheel

The lifeless clay, cold staring, solid mass,
Awaits probing digits, into the block,
The kneading, stretching and pressing to pass

Another rolling maul. Lifted and slapped,
Lashed to the wheel, cupped and centred
To a whirring quadrille, with rising impact?

Did wheel discipline the hand or hand the wheel?
Each shows its commitment to the whole.
Thrown pots rise to full identity.

Spring

Oh spring you have captured my heart again
Taken my eyes for a stroll, begin
Your dance around the countryside
On hill and fen, near and wide
Into the corners did you steal
Of every potted thing and kneel
With nothing but your silvery tongue
The masterly art of life begun

Afterlife

Vexed with the question of afterlife,
Flickering thoughts, a contemplative strife
Furrowed deep in the beaten brow:
At the darkening edges a glistening knife
To lance the very here and now.

Old faces kneel with saintly light,
In burnished pews, deadly - quite
Lips searching for his true meaning:
Rosary clasped in hands good and tight
Between thumb and finger the string passes keenly.

Straddled between now and the great
hereafter. Divine doctrines, tingling faith,
Glorious mysteries and ancient psalms
Steel them. In that moment we cannot dictate
I am what I am.

Section III

Withering away

    withering away
    day by day
    who is to say
    come what may
    withering away
    we turn to clay

Gem

Brimming with bright water
That round her body flowed,
The eyes that were watching her
Blinked to overload

Between the writhing moments
Heady with her perfume,
They rise and fall in unison
Aroused and consumed.

Before the spell was broken
Her eyes filled with blue,
The sacrificial self
Has lived and died with you.

Memories

Memories come gushing,
Unshackled, unrestrained!
Memories together -
Self contained.

Memories come rushing,
Stacked, identified!
Memories forever
Never hide.

Memories come pushing,
Packed, detained!
Memories engender
Life's parade.

And Mother Never Cried

My home of hills and runaway streams
I dream of you still
Beneath the shade of that old oak tree
My childhood schemes were milled
The open fields and country lanes
Where once my heart was high
And little things seemed important then
And mother never cried

The learning days with master's cane
And wishing it was over
To prove yourself to all who said
"He'll always be a rover "
The fishing lines and boyhood dreams
Were cast out in the river
This I guess was growing up
In one way or another

Within the hand of life itself
And countless roads that stretched before me
The yearning for that solo run
Its mysteries and its glory
Had sugared sweet the wanting cries
I knew someday would beckon
"So goodbye to all, I must be off "
Their hugs and all their blessings

Over sea and land I travelled on
And still my heart kept racing
As whistles blew and porters cried
The night was all embracing
Beneath a sky I did not know
And stars that did not greet me
I felt the chilling hand of fate
Rest on my doubts so firmly

I took each day until they took me
Years from when first I came here
Along that path we all must walk
To a future that's so unclear
But these are the chances that make or break
A life that can be so demanding
So get up and get out and run with the wind
And hope for that soft landing

Life

Known by his walk and tortured gait,
He loped along, ungainly, yet straight.

Driven to chase the sparks when they flew,
He grappled with life, what else could he do?

Sentenced to stand at the foot of the stairs,
He often looked up, he never despaired.

And yet when it came to the sinking of wells,
The hazel rod stirred, he knew, he could tell

That life, my friend, winds you up like a spring,
To dissipate, to invigorate, or simply, do your own thing.

Days End

Days end and we separate
Our journey is complete
With one hand on the rocking chair
We cry our self to sleep

That sense of knowing what you are,
The meeting in midstream,
With textured hearts our grasp is strong -
Nothing dents this dream.

The minutes passed with bowed heads,
Pressed and fleshed throughout,
Be on your guard at all times,
So no ones left in doubt.

The contact dwindled with each year
And that's just how it goes:
Friendship can be a fickle thing,
As everybody knows.

Parting

Between the moment of if and when
I sliced into the play
'Til truth limps out and is snared:
Right and left the hanging din
Vapourises my thoughts and leads the way.
Dances with reality, scared.

On tenter-hooks I hang my hopes
To cleave the moments from its prey.
I wrestle to the ground my rising pain.
The solid self wobbles and cannot cope,
Face in hands I cried that day.
Overwhelming thoughts, ramrodding the brain.

The expectation hangs like a mushroom cloud
Permeating each tremulous cell
That cry out why? Oh why?
Hands shaking hands in the gathering crowd
Embracing the sorrow like a tolling bell.
A little piece of me will die.

Resting Places

The pharaohs built big, monumental, colossal sands
Piercing the sky. Sun-bleached stones raised by ancient hands.
Gift wrapped and secreted deep within.
The Anubis jackals guard the fallen king.
Vaulted room, heavy lid, canopic jars.
The heavens swelled with new anointed stars.
Snefru, Thutmosis and the boy king Tut,
Ramesses, Seti; dynasties unmoored and cut
Adrift. And still they dig into that hidden heart
And unearth, hieroglyphic texts, timeless art.
We profile, package, label and tag
Our hoarding hosts, we breathe in sharply and stand agog,
Gold is the flesh of the gods they say.
When Carter broke through he was blown away.
His digging had cast light on that beaten head,
The golden boy in his golden bed.

Section IV

Her Pyramid

Her pyramid. Burnished marble.
Beseeching heaven.
Her life. Quiet and humble.
Posthumous procession.

Her time. Rural idyll.
Humming equilibrium.
Her love. Phosphorus bright middle.
Lifetime speculum.

Her perfume. Seeping regression.
Simultaneous annihilation.
Her hands. Time bombed demolition.
Holistic saturation.

Her death. Lonely journey.
Silent tears.
Our loss. Deep and melancholy.
Dwindling years.

1941

The ink has dried in forty one;
The pressure applied still holds
In anticipation of a rendezvous
Beyond this page, I'm told

Your hand-stitched lines have travelled
On leaves now turning brown;
In grateful appreciation I salute you -
Never one for backing down.

Marooned on your inland island
Holding back the tide,
Suburbia washes up on your shore,
Isolation denied.

You rail against the destruction,
Habitat to habitat;
The countryside was your morning stroll -
You would have died for that.

Your work now only a footnote
In some dog-eared manuscript,
But you had blazed a new beginning,
In the process, took ownership.

Profound Pastimes

I feel it now what I thought was lost
In the vastness of someday soon
To seek me out and fill my heart
With love's elusive bloom

Where I have died there is no cross
For someone to remember
Was it love or should I scream
You gave up you did not surrender

When the moment marries beneath its station
And cries itself to sleep
A new day finds itself divorced
From promises it could not keep

There it goes the afterthought
Looking for attention
When the company it finds itself
Would not give it a mention

The broken lines that make up our life
Teach us one great lesson
No one gets to leave this school
With any hope of re-admission

So let's sit back in our easy chair
And taunt this life with kisses
Maybe just maybe in a moment's thought
Someone might actually miss us

House Martins

They break like missiles from their hornet's nest,
Streaking down the heated air.
Flashed and rapid their burning breasts,
Skimming the land with casual flair.

Roller-coasting around the eaves.
Silent on the steady breeze.
Fighter jets without the boom
Bullet past my living room.

And for a while when they have flown,
I glance up at their empty home.
But they or I have no way of knowing,
Will they be coming or I going?

New Cut Grass

New cut grass
Brings to me
Summer's fresh
Pot pourri.

New cut grass
Wafts the air
With floral notes,
Fresh and clear.

New cut grass
Sets in play
The coming - of
Those halcyon days.

The Millrace

Water! Flowing, running, talking to me
Alongside small timbers turning
Hearken the sound, Oh the sweet silence abides.
Trees talk, looking, I wonder, the miller,
A respected man to his seasoned trade
Wheel embracing, stairs go chasing, chains cascading
Mornings in his eyes before they say…………..

You Are

You are the beauty born of clay
These hands have delivered
Into the fleeting world of self.
Be discovered!

You are the curve that catches my eye
And humbles my artistry,
Laid bare and ill-fitting
Compared to your anatomy.

You are the eyes that bathe me in blue.
Let me go under!
The taste of your lips and caress of your hands,
There is thunder!

You are the vision that fills all my dreams,
My always horizon.
It's moments like these that we should be
Secluded in crimson.

Section V

Shadows Fall

The shadows cosy up to the light
Bright things frighten them
They stretch and lengthen for the fight
Silhouetting Armageddon

Dancing along the perimeter wall
The mottled thoughts seek sanctuary
Throw down your arms once and for all
Lights centuries old adversary

A patchwork of duns, darks and greys
Explodes on the shimmering earth
Cascading waterfalls of light
Incinerates and gives birth

Crass, Crease And Crown

Tippy toe the meadow walk
Thistle tickle tree
Thunder talk a fleshy flight
Forlorn the fiery free
Brittle bough on willow winds
Withstand your seeding soul
Settle soft seduce the cries
Retrieve the ranting roar

Slender songs so lively lit
Summer seasoned sounds
Lantern light lures its prey
Round, round and round
Teasing thoughts through timeless years
Makes it matter most
Never noticing what its worth
Such sentiments are sought

Winning ways it seems you have
For all future fears are fought
Passing, pleasing, playing parts
The numbers not one but naught
Chasing countless carefree capers
Seems such a silly sight
Until the lessons learned at last
Perhaps present trends are trite

Over and over our thoughts are tumbled
Each and everyone explored
Threatened with wisdom the thinking's tiresome
Audacious actions adorned
But believe me when the bubble bursts
Dark days are drawing down
Hero and heroine have had their tale
Crass, crease and crown

Lifeforce

When I look upon you now, blooming.
In this garden of love
I think of the seedling falling
From its height above
Down, down, down among the years
I know the day, I knew the tears
Oh sacred root you have found your home
And to all your gardeners pleasing
I will watch you grow and know that life
Was welling up inside you

Last Summer

When winter has marched this way again
How have I spent my summer?
Can I look back and say
"Ah, it was a time I laughed "
Chased sunbeams 'til they dropped
Their chests heaving with exhaustion
Made treaties with every blossom willing to sign
Heard butterflies chatter in their featherless flight
I was young then not mindful of murderous time

The Dance

It must be said that when we shed
Tears of joy
For one so good I know we should
Our fears destroy

With the dance of time the players swoon
To the mellow thoughts of love
Here in the heart the lutes resound
As the angels sing above
The dance, the dance, the merry dance
Of time, of wine, of light
O sing me please the song of love
I heard on that first night
Sing it soft and sing it sweet
Let it drift up to the stars
To gleam and sparkle for all our lives
'Til our worldly chores discharged

To A Stranger

What pitiful sight, before my eyes
What jagged complexion.
A man, half full with empty, full with hardened pangs
Marked dejection.
How can I help you? With words that don't fill
With tears I can't cry
What then have I!
Less than you that has nothing.
Part we must now for the hour is sank
Down, drown, sour waking.
Merry will be but not without thorning
When thoughts of you in battle are falling.

--------- And death shall no richer be.

Evening Time

Early morning when I rise and shine
I can't wait until evening time

And when I feel myself in decline
I long for the silence of the evening time

That is the one great love of mine
The best part of the day the evening time

ORIGINAL WRITING